Raku

Raku piece by James Fowler; raku piece by the author.

Raku
Art & Technique

Hal Riegger

VNR VAN NOSTRAND REINHOLD COMPANY

NEW YORK CINCINNATI TORONTO LONDON MELBOURNE

Affectionately dedicated to Marion Fosdick

Printed in the United States of America
Drawings by Rae Taub
Photographs by Hal Riegger
Designed by Rosa Delia Vasquez

Published by Van Nostrand Reinhold Company
A division of Litton Educational Publishing, Inc.
135 West 50th Street, New York, NY 10020, U.S.A.

Van Nostrand Reinhold Limited
1410 Birchmount Road
Scarborough, Ontario M1P 2E7, Canada

Van Nostrand Reinhold Australia Pty. Ltd.
17 Queen Street
Mitcham, Victoria 3132, Australia

Van Nostrand Reinhold Company Limited
Molly Millars Lane
Wokingham, Berkshire, England

16   15   14   13   12   11   10   9   8   7   6

On the front cover: Pulling a glazed piece from commercial gas kiln.

Acknowledgments

Many friends have helped this book take form. I am especially grateful to Eleanor Ewing and Fran Smart; and to Frank O'Rourke and Gillian Hodge for reading the manuscript and offering suggestions.

I wish also to thank *Ceramics Monthly* ("Raku," by Angelo Garzio); The Asia Society (*Tea Taste in Japanese Art,* by Sherman E. Lee); The Akasaka Mitoko Company (*The Raku Chawan of Japan*); Transatlantic Art Inc. (*A Potter's Book,* by Bernard Leach); and Universe Books (*Pottery,* by Joseph H. Eppens-VanVeen) for generously letting me quote from their publications.

Finally my thanks go to Lee Ferber and the Ceramics Department and students of Drake University, who were the subjects for many of the photographs in this book.

Preface

Four elements enter into the making of raku: the clay, the glaze, the fire, and the person. Of these the least predictable and most fallible is the person. Raku is a technique; but far more than this, it is also a philosophy. Knowing the techniques is essential, but understanding raku's message permits an ultimate achievement in this extraordinarily simple, yet subtle and complex, craft of the potter.

Many are the areas where imagination and vision must be strong elements, yet equally numerous are the instances where reality must be perceived to provide a balance.

This book is not intended to provide a detailed set of instructions; its purpose is rather to explain the nature of raku. From the information presented, the reader should arrive at his own solutions. More often than not there is more than one answer to a challenge; the response of the individual to the challenges of the clay, the glaze, the fire, and to the moment is the essence of raku.

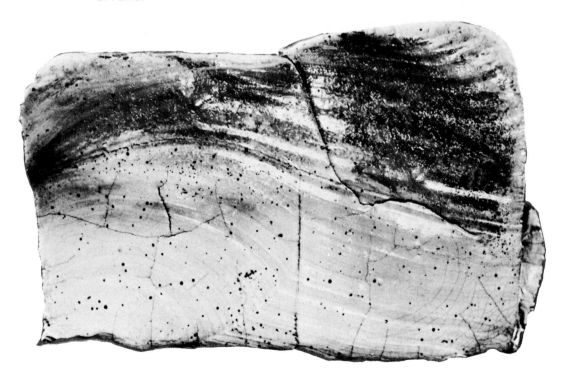

Ice Age, by the author (from 24th Ceramic National). An example of perception at work: a student's cut slab of wedged clay was unchanged, except for partial glazing and firing.

Contents

Japanese raku tea bowl with crackle glaze. *Chikuzen* ware by Sohtchi, early 18th century. (Courtesy of Frances Davidson)

Introduction

Rikyu, a Japanese tea master living in the sixteenth century, is credited with establishing the tea ceremony, a ritual closely tied in with the philosophy of Zen, and one which emphasizes also the beauty of the simple and natural.

One of America's most sensitive potters says of raku: "The cult of tea, or Teaism, is a way of life that expresses an acceptance and veneration of the imperfect in an attempt to imbue man's commonplace surroundings with great meaning and beauty. It places great emphasis on meditation and quiet contemplation as a means of developing awareness of the inherent beauty of the nonperfect, asymmetrical form. It celebrates the excitement of surfaces which derive their character from nature-inspired phenomena; and it becomes a part of the spontaneous creative process, transitory though it may be."

As the philosophy developed, the Japanese abandoned the Chinese *temmoku* bowls they had used for centuries for Korean peasant ware whose simplicity better filled the needs of the new philosophy; but gradually the techniques of raku developed as a response to the demands and ideals of the new form of tea ceremony. Until recently in Japan, raku has been used almost entirely for the making of ceremonial tea bowls. Such was the value attached to these bowls that the shoguns often used them as gifts conveying special honor.

All aspects of the construction of a tea bowl reflect the simplicity and influence of nature in the tea ceremony. When a tea bowl is emptied, a little bit of tea always remains in a shallow depression in the bottom of the bowl. This depression, the *cha-damari,* is supposed to resemble a depression in a rock and the tea in the *cha-damari* to look as "natural as drops of rain in the depression of a stone."

Without many years of experience in the discipline of pottery making and in living within the philosophy of Zen, no potter could be expected to create anything suitable for a function so important as the tea ceremony. (It is with a certain awareness of this and a degree of what I hope is infectious humility that I have even considered writing this book about raku.) Furthermore, the tea ceremony is not part of our cultural heritage. Therefore, the making of tea bowls alone is an unjustified restriction to form that contemporary potters do not always accept. Yet it is well worth noting that within the restrictions of the ceremonial tea bowl form, individuality was, and still is, sought and found. To say that individual freedom is born of certain disciplines is to say, in part, what raku is about.

It will become increasingly evident that our goals in raku are not simply to imitate Japanese potters. In imitation there can be no understanding. Our efforts are to be directed towards understanding those things which are of universal importance.

Pottery is generally, and correctly, understood as the forming from clay of objects that are first fired to harden them, next glazed with certain mixtures of chemicals and minerals, and again fired in order to fuse the glaze. The clay is formed by any one of several hand methods, including the use of the potter's wheel, or by various mechanical methods, such as those employed by industry in mass production. Likewise the application of glaze to a piece may be done by hand, by the studio potter, or by machine, as in the case of the factory. In any case, these operations serve the same fundamental purposes. There are also many variations to these operational sequences. For example, "Bristol" ware is once-fired, glazed pottery, drain and quarry-tile are unglazed products, and there are kinds of dinnerware which may undergo three firings, two of which are for glaze.

Japanese *Cha-wan-gres* tea bowl, 18th century. Reduction spots may be seen on clay under the glaze.

More often than not we are encouraged by professionals and teachers to try to achieve perfection in the Western mechanical sense. Such perfection is a natural goal in a craft inherently fraught with many variable elements, some quite difficult to control. Technology has eliminated some of the difficulties, resulting in greater control and more consistent results. However, along with this have appeared mass production and such phenomena as open stock, where dinnerware, for example, can be matched to customer satisfaction even after a time lapse of many years.

But many potters feel this has brought about a constriction of their attempts at individuality or free expression. Since free expression may well be felt as part of the business of "becoming," in the Oriental sense, is it any wonder that raku is so welcome and favored by potters today?

Raku as presented here is a craft to be mastered through experience and understanding gained through failures, experimentation, and thoughtful inquiry. In no sense can it be undertaken by following prescribed rules or a series of directions; raku's ways are not so specific or clearly defined. In one sense raku is just pottery; it makes use of the same materials, tools, and equipment common to any handmade pottery. In another sense raku is a very special kind of pottery that is as much philosophy as technique.

There are two techniques which differentiate the making of raku from other ways of making pottery. Ordinarily, glazed pottery is put into a cold kiln for firing. The kiln is fired to the proper temperature and is then cooled, after which the finished pieces are removed. The entire operation may take anywhere from six hours to more than a day. In contrast to this, the glaze firing of raku is completed in less than an hour. Glazed pieces are put into a kiln already firing to a dull red heat. When the glaze has fused to the potter's satisfaction, the piece is removed. Metal tongs are used to assist in this operation.

A raku piece remains red hot for a minute or so after it is out of the kiln. In this condition it is possible for the glaze to be modified, both physically and chemically. Alert potters were quick to notice and take advantage of this, and, as a result, they developed certain techniques which result in exotic effects. These techniques were not practised by the traditional Japanese raku potters, but were discovered by contemporary western potters. They are described and discussed in later chapters of this book.

Raku form by William Barnes, combining slab construction with throwing.

Raku box by Robert Brady, enhanced by accidental shattering. The lid was sliced; the interior is carved.

For the mature potter, these special techniques and a knowledge of the ideas which underlie raku make the creation of raku pottery a challenge. While he works, he attempts to create an atmosphere in which the unexpected may happen, and the moment be seized to create a new feeling in form. This in no way implies that the potter tries to cause an accident! Obviously, unexpected things that happen may not all be good. Therefore, part of the discipline of raku is an ability to perceive the difference between good and bad, and the courage to discard the latter.

Potters not familiar with raku will be both disturbed and challenged. Results will occur where there is no precedent for comparison. Was this anticipated, let alone planned? Is it good? What is "good"? These challenges to our visual, emotional, and mental receptivity do not tolerate complacency. The responsibility is ours.

The novice will tend to regard raku's "accidents" as evidence of sloppiness and carelessness. Nothing could be further from the truth. The finest in raku can only be achieved by the disciplined potter; carelessness and sloppiness do not exist in an atmosphere of order and discipline.

Raku piece by the author. Two glazes were used differently on a "found" chunk of clay to emphasize softness on the top and harshness on the side.

In the United States in recent years raku has become known and has attracted widespread interest among potters and teachers. For potters its special appeal may be its philosophy. For teachers the undertaking of raku as an early art experience for students will have its appeal as an exciting, quick, and complete introduction to the fundamentals of ceramics.

Every so often one believes he has come to grips with raku and understands the philosophy associated with it. It is naive for the western mind to think so. One of Japan's highly respected, senior potters was reported recently to have commented that in spite of all his experience and understanding he did not yet feel qualified to meet the special challenges of raku.

On the other hand, social occasions in Japan sometimes take the form of a raku party at which families of status and wealth, along with their guests, will participate in decorating tea bowls. An itinerant potter is employed for such occasions, bringing with him his portable kiln and a number of previously fired (bisque) bowls. Guests decorate the bowls with ceramic pigments, whereupon the potter glazes and fires them.

Is raku so serious, is its meaning so deep as to be fathomless to the western mind? Or is it a game, an enjoyable party pastime? It could be both these things—or neither! If what I have written so far leaves you confused and uncertain, then perhaps I have conveyed the subject rather truthfully.

Zen philosophy may seem one big contradiction to us. Many people have written much about it, but an explanation is difficult, if not impossible.

Raku panel by author of clay pressed onto wood, gravel, and straw.
The glaze was later related to this unexpected result.

The contribution of the raku tea bowl to the tea ceremony is, by contrast to a difficult philosophy, quite down-to-earth. With tea bowls we can respond on different levels to such things as the sense of weight, the feeling of form and texture, the subtleties and unexpected modulations of color, and the pleasure of drinking from a soft, slightly undulating rim. Good raku, whether it be a tea bowl or a different contemporary form, will exemplify these qualities to which any potter will respond.

Raku tea bowl by author, illustrating the play of color and texture from glazed, unglazed, and reduced areas.

Tea ceremony utensils: dipper, scoop, and whisk of bamboo, lacquer tea caddy, two tea bowls, and silk bowl case. The rear tea bowl is by the author, the one to the front is contemporary Japanese.

The Clay

The substance out of which pots are made is clay. However, the term "earth mineral" more accurately describes the actual mixtures used in making pottery. Certain processes in forming and certain characteristics in the finished product will, for both artist and manufacturer, require that various combinations of clay and other minerals be used. There is an extraordinary variety of mixtures, clay and minerals, working properties, and finished product characteristics that prevail in today's field of ceramic production.

The unique techniques of raku subject pieces to severe, sudden heat changes or shock. These differences are in the vicinity of fourteen hundred degrees Fahrenheit. For raku purposes, clays that do not approach maturity (high enough heat treatment to practically eliminate porosity) are generally satisfactory. Also, clay mixtures containing sufficient nonplastic, refractory material and clay mixtures that include minerals of high thermal shock properties are also satisfactory for raku. Because clays vary so in their properties due to their original formation and geographical distribution, it is impossible to give specific recipes for an ideal raku clay. Finding the right clay or mixture is something each potter will have to discover through experimentation.

There are two general ways of coping with the problem of heat shock: Technology can develop heat-shock-resistant materials for use in industry; but primitive people the world over have simply underfired the clay-aggregate mixture. Since raku potters generally use the second method, there is little difficulty in finding a workable clay mixture.

Rarely is a clay found that matures at 1,500°F., the temperature used for raku. Even low-grade brick clays, with their low maturing point, need a temperature of around 1,800°F. to mature them. The occasionally unsatisfactory commercially compounded clay or local clay can be rendered usable for raku by the addition of some high-fire clay or refractory material. Yet even clays with very low maturing points have been used successfully. This is not mentioned to confuse the issue, but to point out that raku cannot be done by rules. There is always a "sixth sense" that prevails.

Natural, unrefined clay, sliced to show coarse material; an ideal type for raku.

Therefore, it must be concluded that, other things being equal, any clay can be used for raku. It can be commercially produced or locally dug; it can be buff- or red-burning; it can be coarse or fine in texture. It is necessary only that the potter have an ability to form and fire successfully good raku pieces with it.

Clays for raku are here listed in broad classifications:

1. *Prepared clays from a ceramic materials supplier* listed in the classified telephone book under "hobby" or "ceramic supplies." These clays are low to intermediate in their firing range, red to white in fired color, and of varied texture and plasticity.

2. *Fire clay or "mortar" clay* is usually sold dry in hundred-pound sacks from local building supply or brick and tile companies. Clays of this type are high-fire, buff-burning, and of varied plasticity, depending upon deposit and type.

3. *Dry, scrap, or pugged local clay* may sometimes be secured from a local brick and tile manufacturing plant. This will usually be a red, low-fire clay, and plasticity and shrinkage will depend upon the type of deposit.

4. *Local, or natural, clays* may be found in the area where the potter lives. These are likely to be similar to brick clays. They have to be searched out, as they are either too small as deposits or too difficult to mine to be useful for commercial purposes. Look for new road cuts, river banks, places where mineral soil has been exposed, and areas where large bodies of water and/or mud have collected and dried. Most often these clays are gritty and considered impure; precisely for this reason, they are good for raku. Many are sticky and easily formed, yet not plastic in the sense that the word defines clay.

The State Geological Survey, the Bureau of Mines, and the Bureau of Mineral Industries (or similar state or federal agencies) usually can supply information about the areas where clay may be found in your state, but often have detailed information only about clays which industry considers valuable. There are many other clays, not commercially valuable for reasons of quality, quantity, or accessibility, that are satisfactory for the raku potter.

Dried clay and rocks along road cut. Cracking is indicative of a more or less plastic substance.

Small clay deposit. Cracks from drying again indicate plasticity.

Water and clay collected in small puddle. Note slimy (plastic) quality at water's edge.

The following is a list of materials, resistant to thermal shock, which may be added to clay.

1. *Grog* (crushed, fired clay) is obtainable from suppliers of ceramic materials or from a local brick plant. Grog is of varying mesh (particle size) ranging from coarse, or 8-mesh, up to fine, or 100-mesh. Depending upon the clay from which it is ground, it will be red, gray, or white.

2. *Sand*, washed or otherwise, may be bought from a local building materials supply store; it is usually sold in fifty- or hundred-pound sacks. Sand may also be picked up from shore or inland deposits. In a raku clay mixture, sand and grog are interchangeable.

3. *Volcanic ash, or pumice,* is a geologically localized material. Certain areas in the midwest (Kansas, for instance) and in the west (Oregon) produce volcanic ash. If available in your area, it would be obtained from either a local building material supply company or a ceramic industry materials supplier.

4. *Talc, alumina or alumina hydrate, and high-alumina clays* have to be purchased from a ceramic supplier.

As in the case of clays, it is of help to refer to a state or federal bureau concerned with ceramic materials.

Clay in normal plastic state.

There is no one correct consistency for clay; rather, its condition must relate to the size and shape of a piece to be made. Sometimes clay must be soft, almost like a paste; most of the time it will be plastic, the condition with which we are most familiar. At other times it must be stiff and almost leather hard (damp but rigid). Often the completion of a piece will require working with clay at several different consistencies. For example: one may wish his piece to have the appearance of pasty or fluid clay. He would start with clay in this condition, pour or spread it onto a porous surface, and wait until it stiffened to a plastic state. He would then lift the clay slab and form it into whatever shape he might choose; at the same time, he would avoid obliterating the slimy clay appearance he originally created. It is all merely a matter of knowing through experience what characteristics different clay consistencies have and how they may best be used in the formation of a piece. Any clay of any consistency is easy to work with so long as its nature is understood and a correct relation established between its physical properties and the piece to be made.

27

There are so many variables in clay working that it is unfair to say clay must be used in only one condition. *All* conditions should be explored to learn how they can be used, which is most compatible with the potter's nature, and which will most adequately convey his message.

Such exploration results, ideally, in the potter's advantageous and creative use of what he observes. Pieces made from nonplastic clay will clearly show the crumbly character of the material both by the forms they take and by the surface quality they reveal. On the other hand, pieces made from a smooth, plastic clay can and should show the smooth, dense, but supple quality of the material. When very coarse, gritty, or even rocky clay is used, this quality must not be hidden, but must be allowed to become part of the total character of the piece. From this it is quite evident that the raku potter has an almost endless selection of types, conditions, and qualities in the clays and minerals from which he can choose to say, in his work, exactly what he wishes.

One's efforts with raku need not be limited to the traditional Japanese tea bowl. What, then, are the possible forms one can make? Esthetic factors will indicate limits, but in all fairness, at this point, it must be said that mechanical (or technical) requirements should govern the form, size, and structure of a piece. The variety of raku pieces illustrated in this book I consider good raku, conforming to the technical demands of the process. Raku procedures suggest that raku pieces be small. Although an assemblage of raku can be almost any size, the individual parts should not be too large, since they will be difficult to handle, especially after glaze firing. But the reader's concept of raku will develop as he reads further about raku methods and practises them.

Attention cannot be too strongly drawn to a correct choice of construction in relation to the character and condition of a clay. Handled sensitively, these elements of pottery working can contribute greatly to the individuality and strength of character in one's work.

Clay almost leather hard: a good condition for carving.

The choice of one's tools also determines and is determined by the nature of the work. What are tools but more versatile extensions of the hands and fingers? Must the potter have specially named tools for pottery or will he discover that a stick and a paper clip are tools? Vendors who tell you it is necessary to purchase "sculpture" or "ceramics" tools only rob you of your right to discovery and invention. Especially in a teaching situation, children should be encouraged to look in the classroom, in the streets, in the home, even in the dump heap to find a wealth of fascinating tools!

Found tools used for impressing plastic clay.

Raku panel by Fran Smart and Hal Riegger, illustrating the use of found tools in achieving an effect.

A common way of kneading clay into a consistent mass.

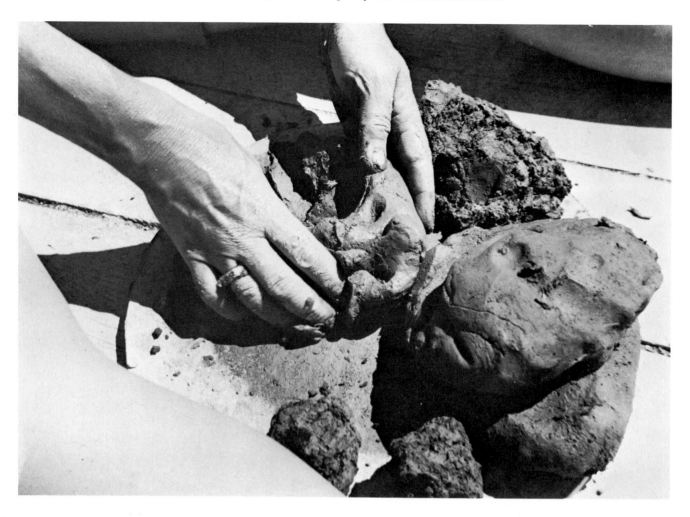

Clay bought in plastic or pugged condition is ready for use unless some aggregate is to be worked into it. In this case, the clay can be treated like bread dough and the aggregate like flour. They are combined through a kneading action, although potters refer to this as "wedging." Raku has repeatedly contradicted the need for one of the precautions usually taught in ceramics—that of wedging the clay carefully to remove air pockets or bubbles. This precaution is absolutely unnecessary in raku, and perhaps in most ceramic work. It has validity, but most often not in the context it is repeated. No air bubble has ever been disastrous in raku, but moisture in the clay has. This example will emphasize the necessity of understanding one's medium rather than blindly accepting everything one hears. This is why I have not drawn attention to the usual precautions and rules about ceramics that most people take for granted. Things about clay working that have no basis in our context, regardless of their source, have been omitted.

An excellent way of wedging clay.

Dry clay absorbs water (slakes) more easily than damp clay, so it is usually time saving to dry the clay first if it is damp. Getting dry clay into a plastic condition is merely a matter of alternately putting water and dry clay into a container that can be covered. The proportion of water to clay varies, but generally is in the ratio of three to four parts of clay to one of water—measurements are by weight and not by volume. If possible, the mixture is allowed to slake a day or more before it is kneaded into a consistent mass. For raku purposes it is usually not necessary to purify the clay by making it into a slip, or fluid state, and screening out impurities.

In pottery everyone's desire is to make a perfect piece the first time. It is highly unlikely any book could assure the reader this kind of success. It is particularly doubtful in the case of raku. I do not agree with the attitude that claims to assure perfect results at the end of a series of prescribed, easy steps. The making of pottery is a creative process. How, then, could there be that delight in one's own discovery, that necessary sense of achievement which gives one a deserved sense of worth and pride in his work, if one is told every step along the way?

Mixing clay and water, and getting the feel of the mix.

Taking Form

Strange as it may seem, nowadays many potters ignore the necessity for craftsmanship in the successful expression of ideas. Subjective "free expression" often seems their only concern. Unfortunately, for those who see only its surface aspects, raku tends to support the belief that ceramics need not be mastered as a craft. But in the work of artists and craftsmen through the ages we see strong evidence of the fallacy of this kind of thinking. Raku may seem simple, yet it need not nourish misconceptions about the position and importance of both craftsmanship and imaginative expression.

Pottery is a complex craft; if raku is accepted as one of its ultimate forms of expression, one cannot presume to learn and master it quickly. In this sense the usual kind of classroom period will not allow much time for developing coordination and facility with materials or tools. Conversely, this very time limitation is compatible with raku's immediacy.

The working environment of a student or potter subtly influences what he does. On a subconscious level people retain modes of conduct, either taught or assumed. They feel there is a certain way to act and think in a studio, for instance. If a working environment can be changed to have less resemblance to what is expected, people are more apt to express themselves freely instead of doing what they believe is expected. In the classroom or studio, whenever possible, it will help to dispense with such things as tables and chairs and with all the other tools and objects normally considered so necessary to pottery working. If it is possible, work outdoors where fences, walls, pavement, and the earth will stimulate the imagination and give wonderful patterns and forms to clay.

Patterns in nature: a granite formation.

Patterns in nature: pattern formed by tide and wind in coastal sandstone.

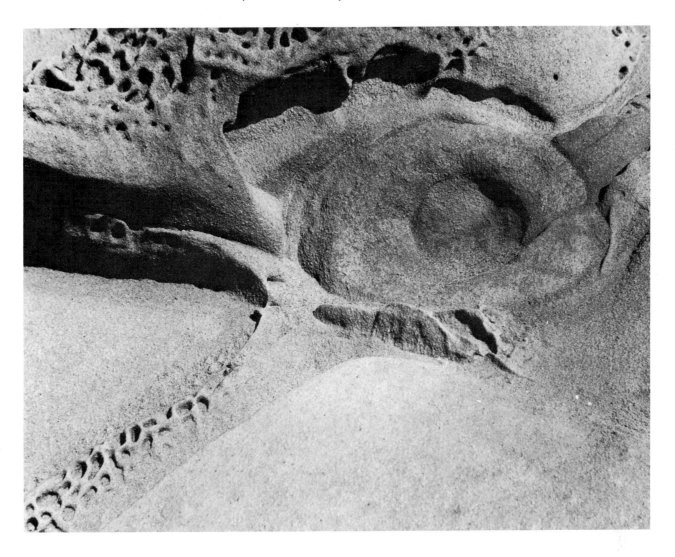

The same holds true with problems in clay. The more unexpected or different from what is anticipated they can be, the more imaginative will be their solutions. Solutions and offbeat challenges are best arrived at spontaneously.

An example of this approach to creativity might be the building of a clay object over, around, and under the table. Another might be the construction of something inside a box. This not only physically supports the clay, but also challenges the person to work in a small, confined area without being able to see the outside of his work. How often do we look only at the outside of a clay piece and not notice what happens inside?

39

Patterns in nature: rocks found along a river bank.

Creating a wood pattern on clay. While the process is similar to Japanese ink rubbings in intent, it is only a partial contribution to the total piece.

Patterns in nature: charred wood slab.

A problem I once presented may not be possible everywhere, but it was a fascinating challenge and typical of what I mean. Pieces of rope, cord, and string of various sizes were tied to the ceiling on hooks. The students were asked to build clay objects on the hanging cords, all of which were short enough so that no one could sit at his work. It is hardly necessary to say that exciting, basic discoveries were made by each person: awareness of gravity, of strength (or weakness) of freely supported clay, the third, moving visual dimension of clay, its mass spinning an unwinding cord.

In many situations the teacher may feel that time limits force him to choose between the experiences of craftsmanship and spontaneous activity. I suspect this is often a rationalization. It is perfectly possible to develop both simultaneously. My own inclination is to schedule the spontaneous encounter first and from this to move to an analysis of the work in terms of mechanics and craftsmanship. I have always felt it was more meaningful to discuss something already made than to theorize ahead of time.

It cannot be too strongly emphasized that raku pieces must be well put together. Construction that might pass for ordinary pottery may well not survive the raku firing. A raku pot made from one piece of clay, without joints, has the best chance of surviving the glaze firing. Some shapes can be made this way, while others cannot. Where several sections are put together, every joint, every place where clay is added to clay, must become no joint at all; the various parts which make up the piece must be unified into a strong whole.

Raku pot by Charles Brown: an example of good construction from two pinch pots with additions.

Clay construction with another material: building a raku pot over a wire cage.

Raku bottle by Carol Hannum. Copper strips are fired into the clay.

When clay sections of the same consistency are put together, the firmest joints will result. However, some forms do not permit this ideal situation, and softer clay may have to be added to firmer clay. If the consistencies at point of contact are made similar, and if the piece is kept damp for a while afterwards, reasonable success can be expected. Roughening and wetting the edge of stiff clay where it will be joined to softer clay reduces the chances that the piece will crack later. Moisture will become evenly distributed throughout the piece if it is kept tightly covered for several days. Then shrinking and size adjustments will take place before the clay becomes rigid.

The low firing point of clay mixtures for raku results in very low shrinkage. The raku process presents one of the few instances in ceramics where other materials, like metals, can be integrated into the clay work and be fired successfully with it.

Limitations to the size and shape of raku pieces exist and may be understood by briefly examining the mechanics of glaze firing. The piece will be placed in a small, red-hot kiln and, upon proper fusion of the glaze, will be removed. Tongs are used to handle the piece and, as the Japanese say, must be used deftly. If for any reason this is impossible, or if damage can occur, the piece has been poorly conceived and the process not understood.

What shapes can the tongs grasp easily? What shapes can be handled without damage? How large a piece can be handled this way? It is necessary to know that, even after firing, the clay will still be fragile or "soft." With experience, both practical and conceptual limits to form and size will be recognized, and there will then be a kind of rightness to the work that respects these restrictions.

After experience with the total raku process, one will become aware of how glazing and subsequent treatment can influence his work. The work will develop with simplicity and strength and will be receptive to the further esthetic complexities of glaze treatment.

Raku plate by author: clay combined with other materials. Nails were imbedded in the wet clay, and bottle glass put on the surface before glaze firing.

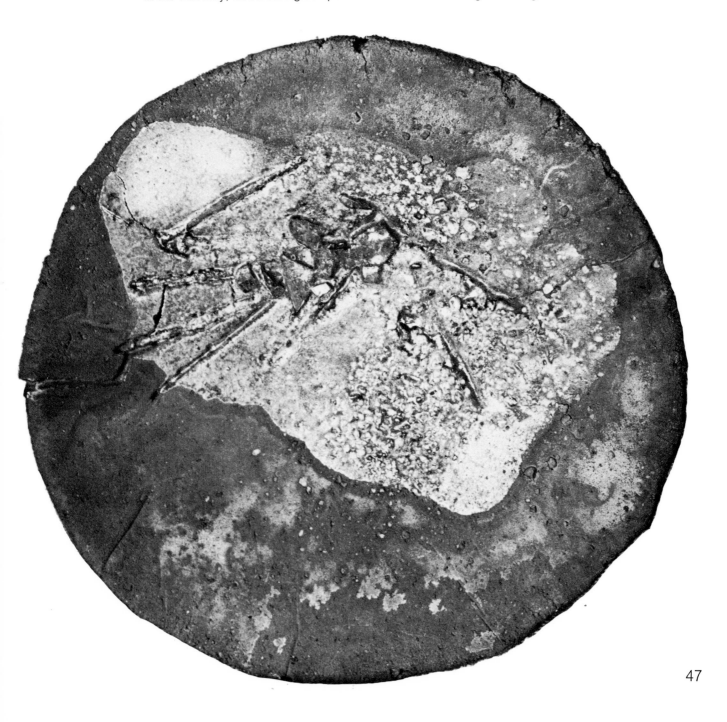

Pots drying on kiln before bisque firing.

Drying

In a classroom situation, it is best to plan the work so that whatever is undertaken can be completed within a single class period. For example, clay mixtures could be prepared and tools gathered during one class. Clay forming and use of tools could be explored in another. Raku pieces are made quickly so that several will be completed in one session. When finished, they must be dried.

At this point the students might be consulted about drying and asked for suggestions about how this might best be done. Presenting problems like this to students for solution encourages thinking and reasoning through which understanding will be reached. Occasionally new answers or methods are discovered—another reason for emphasizing understanding rather than the following of rules.

Pieces are always safe if dried slowly. This can take days, or even weeks: the air drying of common bricks takes several weeks. It is when time is scarce and finished work is to be dried quickly that difficulties may arise.

Clay shrinks when it dries. When it dries unevenly, severe strains can develop, and this sometimes results in cracks.

The most important thing about the final drying of a green (unfired) piece, therefore, is that it be even. (It need not dry slowly, although this helps.) The last part of a piece to dry is usually the bottom, as this rests on a surface where air does not easily reach it.

One way to alleviate this problem is to turn the piece upside down when it is stiff enough; another is to dry it on an open, or perforated, surface; a third way is to place it upon the top of a kiln being fired; there the heat reaches the bottom of the piece first. Kiln-top drying, when and where possible, is an excellent way to dry pieces quickly.

First Firing

Drying a piece of pottery in the air does not really remove all its moisture: pieces often appear dry when in reality they still contain moisture. Thus, the drying process is completed at the beginning of the first, or bisque, firing.

For any bisque firing, including raku, it must be possible to increase heat in the kiln very slowly at the beginning, until the temperature has reached 250°F. or higher.

This process was easily controlled in the small, portable, charcoal-burning kiln used by Japanese potters, partly because of its design and partly because it allowed the potter to control his fire. Saggers (lidded fire clay boxes) were an integral part of this kiln. Ware for the bisque firing was stacked inside the sagger, which acted as a buffer, causing the heat to reach the pottery more slowly. After about four hours of stoking, the kiln attained red heat, and the pots were fired.

The bisque fire offers space-saving advantages. Since no glaze is on the ware, pieces may touch each other without harm. Pieces may be stacked inside of, and on top of, one another. They need only be stacked with care and a consideration of their weight and strength. In an electric kiln, pieces must be kept from touching the elements, and nothing should be stacked against the walls.

Electric-kiln manufacturers recommend leaving the lid and all peep holes open during bisque firing. My own experience suggests doing exactly the opposite. Providing a kiln can be fired slowly, it is far safer to close all openings and create a damp atmosphere inside. This seems a better condition for pots in the early stages of bisque firing, as it allows the pottery to dry from the core out, thus lessening the chances of explosion. By the time a temperature of around 250°F. is reached, dampness will have left the kiln and it will be safe to increase the speed of firing. The kiln can then be fired to the desired temperature and turned off; after normal cooling, it can be opened and unloaded.

Pyrometric cones should normally be used to indicate kiln temperature, unless you are experienced enough to judge it by sight. Cones 012, 010, and 08 are satisfactory indicators for firing raku. If the kiln operates with a pyrometer and automatic shutoff, adjustment should be made within the range of 1,400°F. to 1,600°F.

The raku bisque firing is not intended to produce a high-fired strength in the piece; strength must come from good construction and proper form. Depending upon the clay being used, it may be necessary to experiment with bisque temperatures, but never should they be so high as to mature the clay, making it tough and durable.

Physically, raku bisque pieces are weak and fragile; in the raku context, the word "softness" appropriately includes visual character as well as physical strength. One working in the Japanese context will remember that the quality of softness applies to every step of the work from concept to finished piece.

Intermediate Firing

A haphazard pattern of mottled gray or black with rust occurred on early tea bowls because of the way they were fired. Later the Japanese intentionally repeated this effect.

A wash of yellow ochre is applied entirely, or in part, to a tea bowl either before or after the bisque. Pieces are then fired a second time surrounded by charcoal, in a long fire clay box with a perforated bottom. The fire is started in wood placed under this box, and when a sufficiently high temperature is reached, the charcoal in the box ignites.

It is not necessary to use this technique, but it indicates the opportunities one has for enriching the surface of a piece between bisque firing and glazing. Besides yellow ochre, any of the earth colors and ceramic pigments can be applied and fired onto the piece at this time. There are other minerals and impure, nonplastic clays and silts that might be tried. Information about these substances is included in state publications on clay and mineral resources. In general, the "earths" I refer to may be found in many places just by looking for interesting colors in the ground. However, do not be surprised if these colors change in firing. And remember that many dull-looking minerals can fire to exciting, brilliant terra cotta and brown colors.

Pigment decoration being applied before intermediate firing (underglaze decoration). Note coarse clay.

Pigments to be used in intermediate firing are mixed with water to make a thin wash. If a few drops of corn syrup are added, the mixture will brush onto the surface more easily and will be less apt to rub off in handling. There are no specific proportions for such a wash. Because many of these pigments are strong, and glazes can absorb only a small amount of them, it is safer to make a watery mixture, just as it is safer to avoid more than one application to the piece.

Using pigment on a piece between bisque and glaze firing is not unique to raku. In industry and in the potter's studio this is called underglazing, and the materials used are underglaze stains. What is different in the case of raku is the method of firing the pigments onto the piece. Unless charcoal or some solid fuel touches the pieces while they are hot, it is not possible to obtain such variations in color. To hold this reduced pattern, the raku piece is removed with tongs from the fire and quenched in water; this prevents the reoxidizing, and disappearance, of the reduced pattern.

If the potter can visualize the possibilities glaze offers to his particular piece, he will know whether and how to use pigments at this time. Until you are very familiar with all of the raku procedures, it is recommended that your work be kept simple and bold. The old Japanese glazes were far simpler than ours of today. The many different colors of glazes used today may not only conflict with, but actually obliterate, what lies beneath.

Wheel-thrown raku bottle by Angelo Garzio. Pigment used on shoulder medallion. Finger treatment at base has softened the severity of the wheel-thrown form in raku context. (Photograph courtesy of Angelo Garzio)

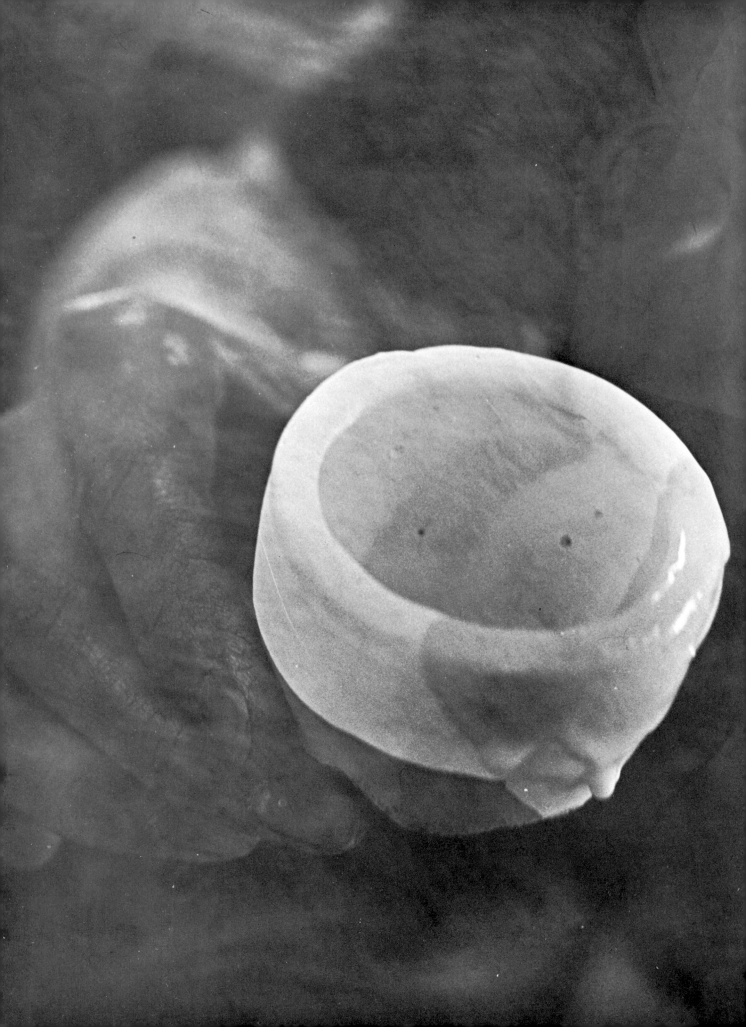

Glazing

There are two types of Japanese raku tea bowls. One is made of a refractory, gritty clay and high fired with glaze made from a particular black rock; in Japan this is referred to as "black raku." The other is low fired and represents the type being dealt with here.

Of the two types, the techniques associated with the latter, or "red raku," are more widely known outside of Japan and form the basis of those used by most potters today.

Basic raku glazes are composed of a limited number of common ceramic glaze materials. Among those are white lead, red lead, silica, china clay, borax, and one or more of several commercially manufactured frits (various specifically formulated ground glasses). Basic glazes can be used as such or may be colored by small additions of ceramic pigments like glaze and body stains, color oxides, and underglaze stains. Temperatures from 1,500°F. to 1,800°F. represent the fusion range of raku glazes being used by potters today.

Raku tea bowl that has been dipped in two glazes to create a pattern.
The glaze thickness is about ⅛ inch.

Raku piece by John Dumas. Excellent combination of glazed and unglazed areas on a piece.

It is recommended that teachers mix their own glazes if they know how and have access to scales and the necessary glaze ingredients. If this is not possible, so-called raku glazes may be purchased from a few companies (The American Art Clay Company of Indianapolis, Indiana, for example). Glazes which are not raku glazes but fuse within the raku temperature range may be purchased from almost any ceramics supplier. But the finished piece will depend not only upon the chemistry of the glaze but, and perhaps more importantly, upon how the potter uses the glaze.

Raku glazes are not fundamentally different from other glazes, yet they have been specifically developed by the potters working in this field. The glazes the studio potter develops are often subtly more appealing than commercial glazes. Newcomers to raku probably will not be concerned with such subtleties, however. Instead they will respond to the immediacy of the glaze firing, and will be excited about the bright colors possible at low temperatures.

We often begin with an image of the finished piece in our mind, and in our inexperienced way go about trying to achieve this; the results frequently are disappointing and we cannot understand why. The potter should instead experiment with tools and materials, like the brush and glaze, to see what they do in their own natural way. From the results of these experiments he can then choose the effects he wants, and he will know how to achieve them.

Often a glaze does not come out the color expected. This can usually be traced to application. Unlike poster paints, acrylics, and other artists' colors, glaze must have body to have color. In raku a glaze that has body will be applied about one-eighth inch thick. Glaze becomes glass in the firing, and only a small part of its bulk, about one-twentieth, is coloring material. Where the glaze is applied thinly, its transparency will reveal the clay color beneath; where applied thickly, the results will be quite different. Thus, a range of color is possible, depending on the thickness of glaze application. Then too, the method of application also influences the character of the finished piece. People using glaze for the first time will often try to get a perfectly even coat by applying glaze with a brush! This is an unthoughtful choice and one that insults the marvelous potential of the brush.

Glazing with a brush will produce certain patterns and effects. A brush is not just a brush: it can be small or large, soft or stiff, pointed or blunt. Whatever its shape or size, it should be loaded with glaze. The brush can make specific bold patterns or it can make a surface of infinitely varied color and texture, but it cannot be expected to produce fine, delicate lines with glaze.

Dribbling glaze with brush: one way to achieve a chance pattern.

A glaze can be applied to a piece very evenly, however, if the method of application is correct. Dipping or pouring is the best way to achieve an even application. While not using much glaze, this method requires a larger amount to work with. It is also a way of producing different glaze thicknesses. These variations are determined by whether the piece is immersed entirely, in part, or several overlapping times.

For making well-defined patterns and line work in glazing, the ear syringe, or glaze-slip trailer, is used. For strength of character, it must be used quickly and with skill. The syringe can produce wavy, zigzag, and tapering lines, or blobs and splats! The pressure on the bulb and the speed with which the syringe is drawn across the clay surface determine the quality of the line, while blobs and splats are formed when air is in the syringe. It is helpful to practise with the syringe on a bare table top in order to become familiar with its potential.

Dipping method of glazing.

Glazing can be an infinitely varied and involved part of the ceramic process; it is far more than just coating a piece. We come closer to an understanding of raku if we consider the pot's surface in somewhat the same way we regard a blank piece of paper or canvas on which to paint. Unglazed parts of the piece are as important as unpainted parts of the canvas in a painting.

The size, shape, and thickness of a piece are closely related to glazing and the results of firing. Besides those aspects of glazing mentioned above, it is important always to think of these four things: How much glaze is used? How does its thickness vary? Where on the piece is it placed? Is more than one basic glaze being used?

Pouring method of glazing.

Raku figure by MaryBell Wilson. Fine example of human character aided by almost casual drip application of glaze.

Depending upon the heat of the kiln, a raku glaze firing will take between fifteen and forty-five minutes. Compared to usual glaze firings, which may last eight hours or more, this is extraordinarily fast. The need to relate piece thickness to glaze thickness to firing time will be appreciated when one considers that the pieces may not have time to heat through evenly. On a piece with considerable variation in thickness, the thinner and more exposed parts will get hot first. The glaze will naturally melt there before it does on other parts of the piece. The skill in glaze firing is to have the glaze melt evenly over all portions of the piece. This is achieved by heating the kiln to a lower temperature and leaving the piece in for a longer time. There are rarely any problems encountered in firing thinly glazed work, but some may occur when the glaze is thick and flows, as it becomes too fluid when the temperature is too high.

Glaze recipes are listed at the end of this chapter. Three have been obtained from the writings of Warren Gilbertson, Bernard Leach, and Joseph H. Eppens-VanVeen. The Leach glaze is authentic and from the First Kenzan, while the Eppens-VanVeen glaze is very close in character to Japanese red raku.

The glazes listed in the recipes range from high-lead to high-alkaline in type. Most are called "basic" raku glazes, meaning that no ceramic pigment is included in the recipe. Several glazes, though, were specifically designed to produce a certain color; these contain either pigments or an opacifier. All will melt within the temperature range of 1,500°F. to 1,700°F., although not necessarily at the same temperature. After working with the glazes, the potter will become familiar with their different melting points and characteristics and will be able to combine intelligently two or more different glazes on one piece.

Raku box by the author. Almost total reliance on unglazed, reduced clay with minimum accent of glaze.

Ceramic pigments may be used with any of the glazes or may replace pigments included in a recipe. The amount of a pigment used in a glaze will vary up to a maximum of about six percent of the dry weight of the glaze. Concentrations that produce what the potter wants will be learned through experimentation. Along with basic glaze ingredients, pigments are listed in order of increasing strength.

New glazes can be developed by substituting one material for another in whole or in part. This may be done easily with the frits, as no drastic change will occur in the melting temperature, but significant changes can occur in character and color.

Hollow raku form by Gillian Hodge. Strong, vigorous symbolism making good use of reduced, bare clay and glaze.

When a raku pot is put into a hot kiln, there is a tendency for the glaze to peel and drop off. This will be eliminated if the glaze contains gum. Arabic, tragacanth, or synthetic gum ("CMC") are all satisfactory. A solution of one-half ounce, or fourteen grams of gum, to one gallon of water is made in advance and used as the only liquid in the glaze.

All raku glazes made in the studio are weighed and mixed with this solution, then screened through an 80- or 100-mesh sieve. If borax is one of the ingredients, it should be kept separate and added to the glaze after sieving.

No specific proportions for liquid (gum solution) to glaze ingredients can be given. Different glaze materials require different amounts of liquid to bring mixtures to a workable fluidity. The potter's preferences and the circumstances also dictate different ratios of liquid to dry ingredients. The very imprecise comparison is often made that glaze thickness should approximate that of heavy cream. Vague as this is, and even though there are other glaze consistencies which are quite workable, it does at least serve as a starting point. Although raku glazes will keep indefinitely, some have a tendency to settle. Adding a few drops or more of vinegar helps to keep them in suspension.

Basic Glaze Ingredients

White Lead
Red Lead
Feldspar
Borax
China Clay
Flint
Ferro Frits 5301, 3124, 3134, and others.*

Pigments

Glaze Stains, Underglaze Colors and Body Stains.*
Antimony Oxide
Iron Oxide
Manganese Carbonate
Copper Carbonate (or Oxide)
Chrome Oxide
Lead Chromate
Cobalt Carbonate (or Oxide)
Tin Oxide

*Various companies manufacture glaze frits, stains, and ceramic colors. Your supplier will secure these if he does not have them in stock.

The frits most commonly used and colors that are readily available are made by: Ferro Enamel Corporation, Cleveland, Ohio; The Pemco Corporation, Baltimore, Maryland; The Glosstex Company, Los Angeles, California; The Ceramic Color and Chemical Company, New Brighton, Pennsylvania; The Mason Color and Chemical Company, East Liverpool, Ohio.

Raku Glaze Recipes

(amounts in grams)

1. Riegger Raku

White Lead	60
Ferro Frit 3124	20
Flint	20

2. Leach Raku

White Lead	66
China Clay	4
Flint	30

3. Eppens-VanVeen Raku

Red Lead	52
or	
White Lead	64
Borax	14
China Clay	4
Flint	40

4. Gilbertson Raku

White Lead	85
Flint	15

5. Riegger Black Luster

White Lead	60
Ferro Frit 5301	20
Flint	20
Copper Oxide	4
Cobalt Oxide	3
Red Iron Oxide	4

6. Riegger Silver White

White Lead	50
Ferro Frit 5301	30
Feldspar	5
Flint	15
Tin Oxide	5

7. Riegger Alkaline Blue

Ferro Frit 5301	50
White Lead	30
Borax	10
Flint	10
Copper Oxide	2-5
Tin Oxide	2

8. 10SR Base for selenium-cadmium reds and oranges (Ohio State University)

Ferro Frit 5301	80
Borax	20
Bentonite	5
Selenium Stain	2-5

9. Modified 10SR

Glostex Frit 625	80
Ferro Frit 5301	15
China Clay	5
Selenium Stain	2-5

Detail of raku plate by the author, showing gravel pressed into wet clay.

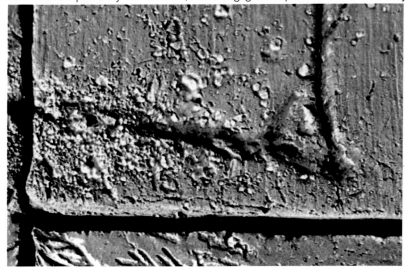

Detail of raku plate by the author, showing cinders fired into clay.

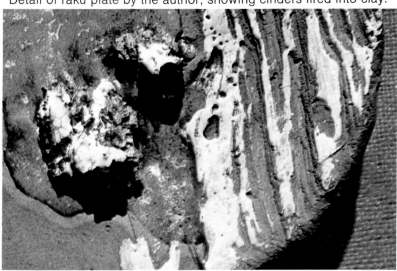

Raku plate by Betty Feves

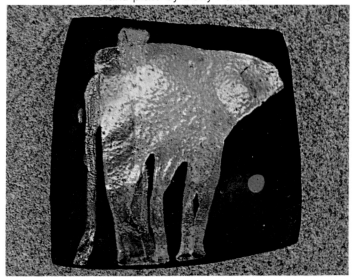

Raku plate by the author.

Kilns

Commercially Made Gas and Electric Kilns

The most common types of kiln in use are gas fired and electric; both are suitable for firing raku glazes. Either a top-loading kiln with a hinged lid or a side-loading kiln with a hinged door may be used. It must be possible to open and close the kiln often without harming it. Of the two types, a top-loading kiln is more convenient for raku glaze firing.

Ideally, all dimensions of the kiln interior—height, width, and depth—should be the same and range from six to twelve inches. Kilns of this capacity will accept most raku pieces.

If only a larger kiln is available, adjustments can be made so it will better suit the needs of raku firing. With top-loading kilns it is customary to reduce the depth, making a false floor from shelves supported solidly on several bricks. With front-loading kilns the mechanics of alteration are a bit more complicated, but certainly not impossible. Kilns come in such a variety of shapes and sizes that each will present its own problems. One must be sure always that in an electric kiln nothing blocks the elements, and in a gas-fire kiln nothing hinders the normal, free circulation of flames.

Raku bowl being removed with tongs from an electric kiln.

Japanese-type wood-burning kiln in operation. Note red heat at top.

Interior of wood-burning kiln during firing.

Some kilns of standard front-loading design that are not commercially built have bricked-up doors. They may easily be adjusted for raku firing. After the location of the opening is determined, a false floor is built at this level and the door bricked up to this point. The most easily handled raku door is a single insulating, or standard fire clay, block; its hole will be large enough to accommodate the ware being put into the kiln, or about nine to twelve inches square. If neither is available, a heavy piece of metal, properly fashioned, might work satisfactorily at raku temperatures. The remainder of the regular kiln door is bricked up around the raku door, leaving enough space to allow for easy removal of the blocks; mortar is not used.

Noncommercial gas-fired kiln modified for raku firing. Rarely would a kiln this large be used for raku, but the method of adapting it to use only a small part of its capacity is illustrated here. Three piles of bricks support the working shelf (for clarity, only the bottom bricks are shown).

Raku tongs which open to six inches.

The maximum temperature to which any kiln can fire is unimportant, because even those with the lowest rating, such as enamel kilns, will fire to raku temperatures.

Kiln design, partly, determines the best kind of tongs to use. Pieces fired in a top-loading kiln are grasped vertically, at the top, where a rim or other thin area exists, so tongs do not need to open wide. Where pieces are placed into a side-loading kiln, they must be grasped in their entirety, and tongs which open wider must be used.

The Japanese potters have a high regard for tong marks left in the glaze. But, as honest evidence of the process, they should show deft handling of the tongs!

Raku firing can be hard on a kiln, and certain advance preparation will prevent damage. Sometimes glaze will flake off or drop from a piece and melt onto the floor. An old kiln shelf may be used to protect the kiln floor, but, if one is not available, a new shelf may be substituted. The shelf should be given a good coat of kiln wash and set above the bottom, allowing one or two inches of space beneath it. Asbestos transite also provides a protective coating for shelves and can be discarded after it becomes dirty. Shelves should be cleaned after each glaze session and, if necessary, rewashed before the next one. Kiln wash can be purchased from your ceramics supplier, or made into a thick fluid from equal parts of china clay and flint mixed with water.

82

Gas kiln ready for raku glaze firing. Raised shelf insures heat at bottom of pot for even firing. Note old shelf on bottom to protect the kiln floor.

After glazing, and before firing, it is necessary to dry the piece completely, over heat. Unfortunately, every so often a damp glazed piece gets into the hot kiln and explodes. If this happens, the kiln must be turned off immediately and cleaned out as soon as possible. Any glazed fragments touching elements should be carefully knocked off with a heavy wire or rod so permanent damage does not occur. Shattered pieces are removed with tongs. When the kiln has cooled enough, shelves, supports, and rubble should be taken out. Fine pieces are best sucked out with a vacuum cleaner.

Kilns of the sizes mentioned can be heated quickly, but larger ones will be heated more slowly; as far as raku is concerned, it makes no difference. It is only necessary to be certain that the kiln structure is not weakened by quick heating and expansion of its parts. Normally it will not take a small kiln longer than one or two hours to reach working temperature.

Surfaces immediately in front of, and to the sides of, the kiln should be fireproof, or protected with some nonflammable material. Pieces coming from the kiln must often be set down and picked up again for easier handling. It is practically essential to have bricks, kiln shelves, asbestos, or metal around the kiln for safety.

Variation of portable charcoal kiln used by Japanese potters. Note sagger and glazed pieces drying on the rim.

Noncommercial Wood, Charcoal, and Gas Kilns

Experienced raku potters generally prefer kilns they have designed and built. Each potter has his own preferences about firing; his reasons for building his own kiln are control of heat and kiln atmosphere, accessibility for glaze firing, and the pleasure of total involvement.

The glaze firing, the kind of kiln, and the way it fires all contribute to the character of a raku piece. As mentioned earlier, one of the most important elements of the character of raku is softness; wood and charcoal kilns of Japanese design cannot easily be fired too fast or too high and are therefore gentle to the ware. If it seems that I am partial to these kilns, I am. While I realize it is often impossible to have and use wood-burning kilns, I urge that they be used whenever circumstances allow.

Gas- and oil-fired kilns, particularly those aided by blowers, can be fired fast and to high temperatures, but an ever-present audible reminder of a technological force intrudes on the potter's senses. To me it is an adverse influence, unacceptable to the experienced and dedicated raku potter.

Raku saggers, lid, and plug. Note grooves for soft iron wire reinforcing.

The several kilns illustrated and described here function with varying degrees of efficiency. Some are easily built, while others take more time and skill; some waste fuel, while others use it more efficiently.

The original charcoal- and wood-burning kilns of Japan demanded the use of a sagger—a clay pot in which the pottery is placed for bisque and glaze firing. While the sagger is still mandatory in charcoal kilns—to prevent the flaming charcoal from touching the pottery—it has become, in the last few years, optional in the wood-burning kilns where the simpler kiln shelf is now often used. The choice is the potter's and depends largely on whether or not he wants to buy or make a sagger.

Saggers may be purchased from certain manufacturers (such as the Louthan Manufacturing Company of East Liverpool, Ohio). But any sagger from such a source would be costly and might not suit the needs of the raku firing. One made by the potter himself is more satisfactory in practically all respects.

A well-constructed, hand-built sagger will last longer than one made on the potter's wheel. It should be between nine and twelve inches in diameter and height, and not more than one-half to five-eighths of an inch in thickness. A mixture of fire clay and sand or grog in a ratio of two to one or three to one and made up to plastic condition should be used. All joints must be well made.

Since even the best saggers do not stand constant heat changes very long, provision should be made to hold them together with soft iron wire. Lid design, and grooves around the sagger, as shown, permit wire to hold the parts together serviceably long after they have cracked.

After drying, saggers, lids, and plugs are best fired to a moderate bisque of about cone 08 or 06. If a kiln is not available for this, the raku kiln itself can fire them. If this is the case, the kiln must be fired very slowly and carefully; four to five hours of gradual heat increase will not be too long a time to reach the right temperature. For this firing the wood-burning kiln is fired hotter than for the subsequent glaze firings. To indicate temperature, for this firing only, cones may be placed inside the sagger and observed through the plug hole.

Attaching first strip to bottom.

Making a firm joint between strips of sagger wall.

Finishing rim and interior.

Variation of Japanese wood-burning kiln.

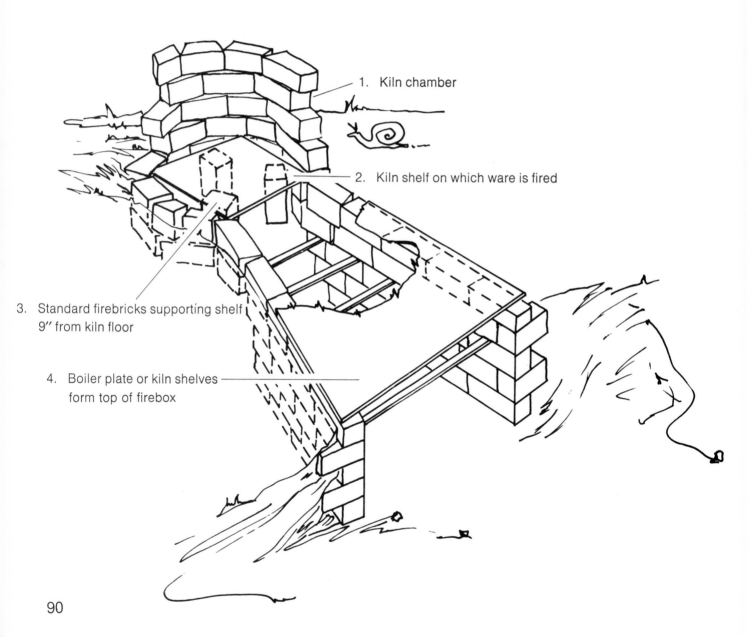

1. Kiln chamber

2. Kiln shelf on which ware is fired

3. Standard firebricks supporting shelf 9″ from kiln floor

4. Boiler plate or kiln shelves form top of firebox

90

Traditional Japanese Wood-Burning Kiln

The accompanying drawing illustrates the important elements of design and proportion of the traditional Japanese wood-burning kiln. A kiln of this design, like any kiln, may or may not perform well the first time, and it will be sensible to build it so that structural changes can easily be made.

The accompanying photographs show this type of kiln built into a bank, which has the advantage of support from the earth.

In one form of this kiln, a sagger is used. Here the most critical dimension is the space between the sagger and the adjacent kiln wall. If the sagger is approximately ten to twelve inches in diameter, the gap for flame passage is one and a half to two inches. Less space will choke the fire, while more will waste heat and fuel.

The second most important part of the kiln design is the ash pit, where coals and ashes collect. Experience has shown it must be larger than would be expected, or roughly twice the capacity of the firebox. Primary combustion air enters the kiln here, and provision should be made for controlling it by means of an adjustable door.

A slightly modified version of this kiln uses a kiln shelf in place of the sagger. To minimize the effect this change has on vertical evenness of heat, it is advisable to extend the structure upwards six inches to one foot. Aside from eliminating the need to make a sagger, this kiln offers the potter the advantage of being able to see his piece at all times during the firing. Building this type of kiln into a bank provides structural support and insulation, but since movement around the kiln may cause ashes and dirt to fall onto the ware, the potter must be careful in his work around the kiln.

A second variation of the Japanese kiln is a solid fire-clay sand arch over the firebox. There is more work involved in its construction, but with this kiln one avoids dependence on materials like boiler plate, which are sometimes difficult to obtain.

Ash pit and base of kiln chamber have been completed.

Walls of firebox are being added.

Start of circular kiln chamber and completion of firebox top with
16″-square fire clay slabs.

95

Continuation of kiln chamber with kiln shelf floor in place. Note that floor is level with firebox top.

Completing the kiln chamber. Note firebox grate.

Japanese-type wood-burning kiln on level ground. Solid firebox arch made over aluminum form from clay-sand mixture. Note brick facing supporting sheet metal door.

An arch as long as the firebox is made of sheet metal, preferably aluminum, corrugated or sheet roofing. It is supported in place by blocks of wood or bricks so the base of the arch is level with the next-to-top row of brick in the firebox walls. A mixture of fire clay and sand or grog is mixed somewhat drier than for saggers and may contain even more sand if desired. The mixture is built over the metal arch to a thickness of four to six inches and rests on top of the firebox walls. A brick facing can be made to facilitate support of the sheet-metal firebox door. The fire-clay mixture should be stiff enough, ideally, so that it will have to be tamped in place with bricks or wooden blocks, thereby making a solid, dense arch. The arch does not need to be air dried; a fire can be started in the kiln immediately. It will be found that, a few hours after the fire has begun, the aluminum form will melt into the firebox (it can be removed later), and the fire-clay arch will remain.

Working temperatures in these kilns are reached in two to three hours. Firing conditions improve as the kiln becomes more thoroughly heat-soaked; best results in firing usually come at the end of a day's run.

97

Japanese-type wood-burning kiln: a variation.

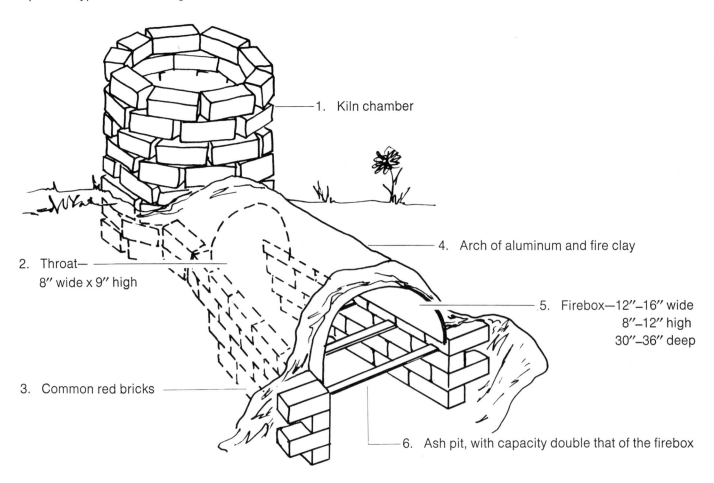

1. Kiln chamber

4. Arch of aluminum and fire clay

2. Throat—
   8″ wide x 9″ high

5. Firebox—12″–16″ wide
   8″–12″ high
   30″–36″ deep

3. Common red bricks

6. Ash pit, with capacity double that of the firebox

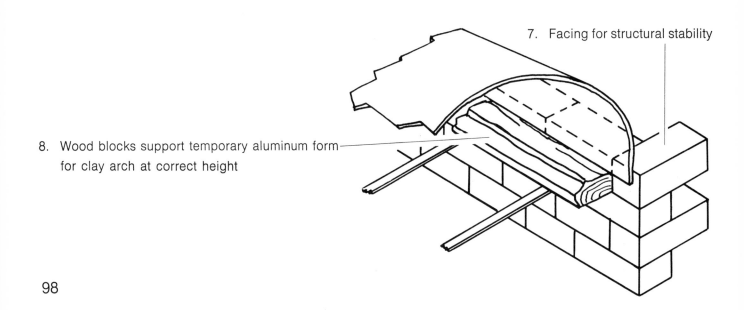

7. Facing for structural stability

8. Wood blocks support temporary aluminum form
   for clay arch at correct height

Portable Japanese Kiln and Modified Versions

Because this kiln is carried by itinerant potters, it has to be small and light. Hot-burning natural charcoal that takes little space is used for firing. It can be built as a portable or permanent kiln, although each will require somewhat different materials. While the small, lidded sagger is common to both, the surrounding walls are different.

The containing walls of the original portable raku kiln were constructed as one unit of fire clay and grog. Combustion holes about two inches in diameter were evenly spaced around the circular wall. After firing, and before the kiln was used, this fire-clay drum was banded with three or four metal strips to hold the unit together in case it cracked.

With this kiln, as with the others, the sagger dimensions of ten to twelve inches are the starting point upon which the remaining dimensions are based. Space needed for burning charcoal is about four inches between the sagger and the kiln walls, making a diameter of approximately twenty inches for the kiln drum. Three piles of bricks suport the sagger about six inches off the kiln floor.

A modified, nonportable version of this kiln is illustrated following. It is similarly built, but with a metal shell, and it is lined with insulating fire brick.

A second modified version, also nonportable, has walls made of brick, on a brick base, with gaps in the walls for ashes and combustion as follows: the bottom two rows should provide four to six holes approximately four inches wide for ash removal (during firing, bricks are used to plug these holes); each row above this up to the level of the sagger top should provide about four holes for combustion, each about two inches wide, in a staggered pattern. Less space is required for combustion and ashes when burning charcoal than when burning wood.

Charcoal is usually available in two forms; of these, natural hardwood charcoal is preferable to briquettes, although the latter are frequently used. During firing, fuel should be added as necessary to keep it level with, but not above, the sagger rim. By contrast to wood-fired kilns, heat does not extend up and over the sagger top; for this reason, pieces not more than about two-thirds the sagger height will fire best. This kiln takes longer to reach working temperature than the wood-burning kilns, generally about three to four hours.

Portable Japanese fire clay kiln casing, with metal strap binding—20″–24″ high x 16″–20″ diameter.

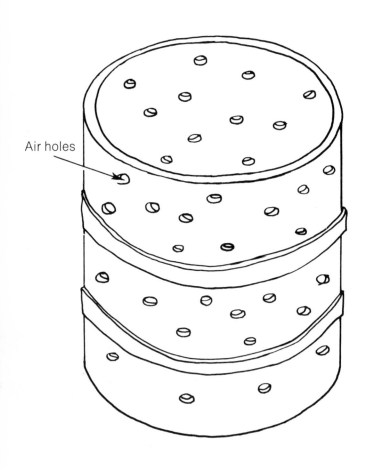

Air holes

Modified version of portable kiln, using metal shell and insulating firebricks.

Charcoal

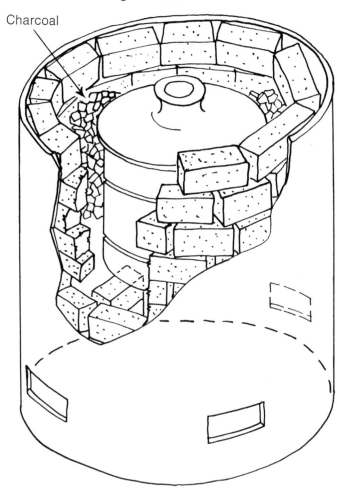

Fuel fill line   Fuel chamber

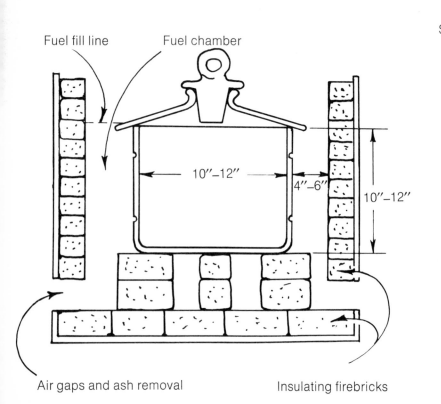

10″–12″

4″–6″

10″–12″

Air gaps and ash removal   Insulating firebricks

Soft iron wire wrapped here

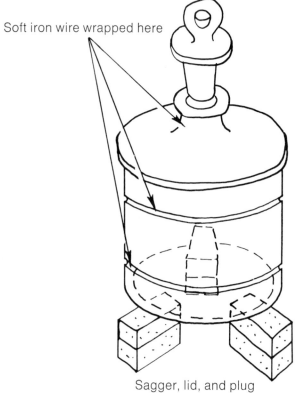

Sagger, lid, and plug on supporting brick

Permanent Japanese-type charcoal-fired kiln. Hooked rod is used for pulling sagger lid plug. Note wire reinforcement around hole of sagger lid.

Stationary Wood-Burning Kiln

This kiln is an adaptation of the nonportable Japanese charcoal kiln. Its design differs in its increased space for burning wood, and the absence of combustion holes above the bottom two rows of wall brick. Space between the sagger and the surrounding wall should be at least six inches, and the sagger should be supported six to eight inches off the kiln floor on three piles of bricks.

The advantage this kiln offers is its easy, simple construction; fire regulations permitting, it can be built anywhere. A few of its disadvantages are greater fuel consumption, the need for greater cooling than other kilns when pieces are changed, and an interior less easily seen during firing. It also takes more care and skill to stoke this kiln; uncontained flames may reach upward as much as a foot at times. Working temperatures are reached within one to two hours, more quickly than in the previously described kilns.

Despite certain drawbacks, this kiln is recommended for those unfamiliar with more complex kiln construction and where it will not be considered a permanent structure.

Stationary wood-burning kiln, 20″ high, 7–8 bricks per layer.

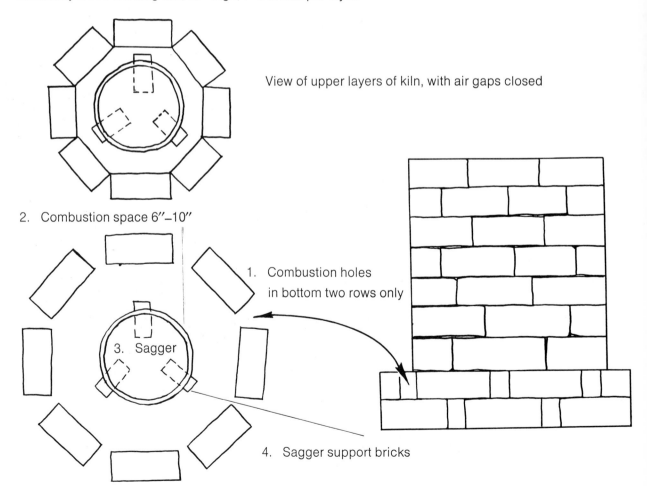

View of upper layers of kiln, with air gaps closed

2. Combustion space 6″–10″

1. Combustion holes in bottom two rows only

3. Sagger

4. Sagger support bricks

Stationary wood-burning kiln. Note air gaps only in bottom two rows of bricks.

Floor construction used in experimental wood-burning kiln.

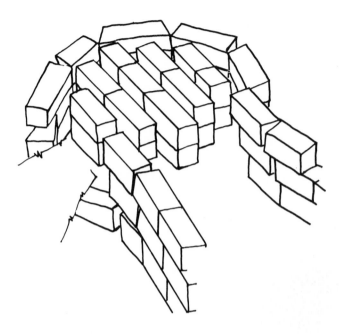

Some Experimental Kiln Designs

Other modifications of Japanese raku kilns are illustrated here and described briefly. They are all small, updraft, and designed for easy interior access.

One kiln differs from the traditional Japanese kiln only in the construction of the surface supporting the ware to be fired. It was built during a workshop where only common bricks, a few firebricks, and some sheet metal were obtainable. It is illustrated to show how potters can innovate when they understand basic principles.

No shelf or sagger was available, and time did not permit making either; instead, firebricks were placed on edge, three-high, in spaced rows. Gaps between the rows paralleled the kiln lengthwise, allowing flames to enter the kiln chamber and pass under and around the ware. This part of the construction occupied the bottom of the kiln chamber up to the normal level of the sagger bottom, which is the same level as the firebox top. The kiln functioned well, but because of the greater mass of the floor, took longer to reach working temperatures.

View into experimental wood-burning kiln through chamber, showing firebrick floor.

Mills College kiln, using gas and forced air.

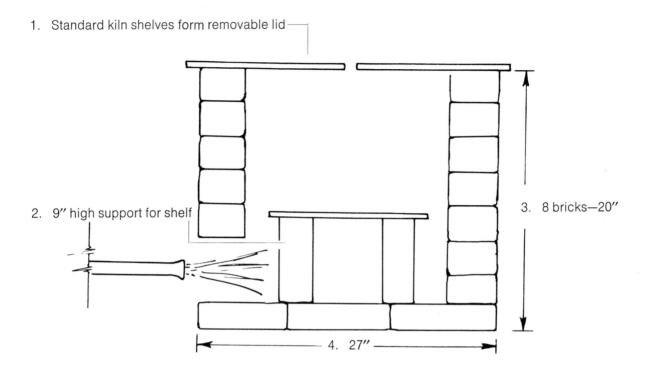

1. Standard kiln shelves form removable lid

2. 9" high support for shelf

3. 8 bricks—20"

4. 27"

When gas is used for fuel, the kiln can be smaller and simpler in construction. The kiln illustrated here was built by students at Mills College during the winter of 1968–69. It is a cube of standard firebrick. Two sillimanite shelves form the removable top, and a sillimanite shelf on several strategically placed bricks forms the inside floor on which ware is fired. The burner consists of a controllable gas supply in conjunction with a small vacuum cleaner blower—air and gas, moving through a pipe about twenty-four inches long, are blended into an efficiently burning mixture. As long as they are large enough, the size of the spaces under and around the shelf inside the kiln is not critical.

Whenever a concentrated fuel such as gas is used, there is a tendency to let the kiln overheat, causing glazes to bubble and flow. I have noted repeatedly that people seem unaware of the high heat potential of gas and forced air; they tend to forget that the burner must be turned down considerably once working temperature in the kiln has been reached.

Materials Needed for Kiln Construction

Materials for the Traditional Japanese Wood-Burning Kiln (quantities approximate)

Sagger (with lid and plug)
3 standard firebricks (throat arch)
200–300 common red bricks
4–8 grate bars (1″ reinforcing iron or angle iron)
Firebox cover: several 18″ or 24″ by 12″ kiln shelves or ¼″ boiler plate of adequate size
Firebox door: sheet metal with wire loop handle

Materials for the Japanese-Type Charcoal Kiln and Stationary Wood-Burning Kiln (quantities approximate)

Sagger (with lid and lid plug)
80 common red bricks

Firing the Kiln

Since heat is the product of the combustion of fuel and oxygen, it follows that adequate oxygen must come into contact with a fuel for it to burn efficiently. To achieve good combustion, the kiln door will have to be adjusted during firing.

In the early stages of any firing, only a small amount of heat is wanted. As the firing progresses, more and more heat is necessary to increase the kiln temperature to its desired heat.

Thus, at the beginning of a bisque firing, relatively large pieces of wood (hard wood is preferable, but not necessary) are used in the firebox. Sometimes these may have to be ignited outside the kiln in a small fire and then inserted into the firebox, where they may hardly do more than smoulder. After 212°F. is reached, the rise in temperature can be speeded up. Wood of smaller and smaller size is used as greater kiln heat is sought, until, at the end, when maximum temperature is achieved, finely split wood is used. In the case of a raku glaze firing, when the desired temperature is reached, fuel consumption is lowered, since now it is only a matter of maintaining temperature. At this time the fire will have to be stoked as often as every two minutes, but with only a very few sticks of wood each time.

Mills College kiln showing burner made of fire clay tube which blends gas and forced air.

Splitting wood for hotter fire.

Stoking Japanese-type wood-burning kiln. Note lack of smoke.

Looking into incandescent kiln; pieces are ready to be removed.

Glaze Firing

While there are necessarily differences between glaze firing in commercial and noncommercial kilns, the principles involved are the same, and the subject can be treated in one chapter, with attention being drawn, where necessary, to the differences or variations in techniques. One advantage of a wood-burning kiln is that it provides room on its rim for glazed pieces to dry quickly before firing—it does not matter if the pieces become sooty or the glaze begins to melt. The potter must learn how to hold the kiln temperature for soaking, and how to build up lost heat, slowly or quickly, as the situation demands; this is more difficult with wood- and charcoal-burning kilns.

It cannot be emphasized too strongly that the kiln is a versatile tool to be used in a variety of ways. Kilns are just as individual as people, so knowledge of the kiln, through intelligent and repeated use, permits the potter to gain the most from it.

Glaze firing is a dramatic part of the raku process. It demands skill, complete attention, and almost split-second timing. The contradictory nature of the situation is demonstrated when calm and composure must walk hand-in-hand with the excitement attending this red-hot happening. Glaze firing raku is something you never let someone else do for you!

Raku glaze firing brings the potter face to face with a new experience. Certainly he has fired kilns dozens, perhaps hundreds, of times, but until his first experience with raku he has not been able to see what happens inside. A solid brick barrier has separated him from his firing pots; now they are in full sight. Because he may open the door or sagger lid as often as he wishes, he can see the glaze fusion as it progresses, he can touch the pot, and he can do things to it which are impossible to accomplish in any other firing situation.

Here are some ways in which a potter can influence his pieces: because he sees what is happening to the glaze, he can stop its progress at any moment he chooses; with a fuel-fired kiln he can quickly change the atmosphere from oxidizing to reducing, thereby influencing glaze and clay color, and possibly altering glaze texture; he can add another dimension to the pot's surface by dropping or blowing some material into the firing pot—something that may or may not fuse at the kiln's temperature (borax and sand are two possibilities). These are but a few of the opportunities presented by raku glaze firing.

A glazed piece put into the kiln when it is started will show when working temperature has been reached; when the glaze has melted properly, the kiln is hot enough to accept further pieces. The only safe time to put a damp piece into the kiln is when it is cold. As temperature increases, the piece may be watched through peep holes or by opening the door. When the glaze appears to have melted properly on a piece, it is removed and replaced by another. Once the potter learns the kiln's firing pattern, he will not need to look into it early in the firing. Later in the firing a piece must be carefully watched because a few minutes one way or the other can make quite a difference.

Ideally, one piece is placed in the kiln at a time in such a way that its different surfaces are visible. It is a common error to place a piece so that only its top can be viewed. Glaze may have melted properly here, but when the piece is taken from the kiln, other surfaces are found not to have melted adequately. For instance, glaze tends not to fire evenly on tea bowls, although they are the pieces with the most consistent wall thickness in raku. But the glaze will melt first on the rim and last on the inside bottom. Often it will be necessary to leave the piece in the kiln longer, maintaining, but not increasing, the temperature, in order to fuse the glaze everywhere on the piece.

The potter must think ahead to the time when he will take the piece from the kiln. To do this quickly and at the right moment means the piece must be put into the kiln correctly. This is especially true of flat objects (such as tiles) more easily handled vertically by their edges. If they cannot be fired leaning against the sagger or kiln wall, a small chunk of brick under one edge will make them accessible to the tongs. The brick is put in the kiln in advance so that it will get red hot and not retard glaze fusion anywhere on the piece.

Thinly glazed pieces are easy to fire. Often, potters use a thin glaze on a rough surface and misinterpret what they see in the kiln as an under-fired glaze. What they usually see is rough clay showing through a well-fused but thinly applied glaze. The clay surface of a piece must therefore be remembered when a thinly applied glaze is fired; in the kiln the clay texture will be more evident than the glaze surface.

114

Glazed pieces being removed from a gas-fired kiln.

A thickly glazed piece presents a different firing situation. Greater attention and control of the kiln is necessary. As noted before, there is a tendency for potters to have their raku kilns too hot; glazes fired too quickly and at too high a temperature will bubble and flow at the same time. When this happens, the piece may have to be discarded. To avoid this kind of mishap, the firing should be done at somewhat lower temperature and for a longer time.

The potter must also know that different raku glazes do not all melt at the same temperature; their fusion points, covering a range of several hundred degrees, were mentioned earlier. Therefore, he must use good judgment when he applies more than one glaze to a piece.

Like any glazes, raku glazes undergo changes as they get hotter. In the first stage the glaze sinters; then it becomes buttery soft. Many potters consider this the ideal way to fire raku glazes. The next stage causes the glaze to bubble: you will notice great activity on the surface. Most bubbles will remain and harden if the pot is taken from the kiln at this point. In the next, and final stage, the bubbles have left the glaze and it is in a very fluid state. It has not only pooled in depressions but has run on vertical surfaces. Its hard, glassy feel will be similar to that of commercial glazes, a quality not particularly sympathetic with the soft character of raku.

No doubt someone will produce a beautiful raku pot that contradicts this statement. Knowing these things, a potter must make his own decisions about how to fire a glaze. What will emerge is a concept of raku that is his own.

When both kiln and piece are red-hot, it is hard to see how the glaze is melted. This phenomenon, called immiscibility, refers to the difficulty of discerning surfaces, details, and sometimes objects when the kiln and its load are incandescent.

One can see progress of glaze fusion in a wood-burning kiln by getting something bright to reflect off a piece. Japanese raku potters drop a straw into the kiln to see its flame reflected. In an electric kiln the elements are always glowing hotter than what is in the kiln, and from the right angle of vision they can be seen reflected from the glaze surface. For some people accurate evaluation of the glaze condition will be possible only in daylight, out of the kiln, when a quick survey of all surfaces can be made. If the glaze has not been sufficiently fired, the piece can be put back into the kiln.

Cones are not used in glaze firing. Since many pieces are successively fired over a period of time, the cones would be of no use after they had melted when the first piece was finished. The main reason for not using cones, though, is that there is no one correct temperature for glaze firing; a potter will choose to fire a given glaze differently from time to time.

Provided the firing has produced the desired glaze quality, the piece is removed from the kiln. Several things can now be done to it. The piece may be left to cool in the air until it can be handled. It may be plunged into water, which is said to soften the glaze texture; if this is true, however, the change is so subtle as to elude all but the most experienced observer.

There are other, more complex ways of handling pieces after they come from the kiln and these have greater effect on color and appearance. They are described in detail in the following chapter.

After Glaze Firing

Traditional air- and water-cooling of raku pieces are rarely used by potters today. Instead, in one way or another, they are reducing pieces, an exotic treatment producing all kinds of marvelous changes. It is my belief that this treatment is not traditional and represents a misinterpretation of the function of the intermediate charcoal firing. But regardless of its origin, it has been an important contribution to ceramics and has extended both the technique and concept of raku. The techniques of reduction are not new. Reduction obtained through the contact of a red-hot piece with combustible material outside the kiln was practised centuries ago in the Lower Congo and by the Ashanti, although as far as I know, glaze was not involved.

Reduction is usually thought of in connection with high-fire stoneware, and as practised with raku is theoretically not too different. The physical circumstances are different, however—the time is less, and the temperature much lower. The effect is therefore only on the surface, and the appearance of reduced raku ware can in no way be likened to that of stoneware.

Described simply, pieces are put into an atmosphere lacking oxygen at a time when they are responsive to chemical change. The former bisque color of clay will change to gray or black; glazes containing copper, for example, may develop a surface luster changing from a blue-green to an iridescent red or metallic copper color. It is interesting to note that in the latter case the surface will tarnish and can be polished in the same manner as metallic copper. As regards the effects of reduction on some raku glazes, the results are similar to low-fired luster glazes.

To sum up, a raku piece must be reduced in the presence of an atmosphere lacking in oxygen and containing free carbon. How this condition is created and the length of time it influences the pieces are factors controlled by the potter.

119

Reduction using wood chips.

Combustibles such as sawdust, straw, paper, leaves, and charcoal are used. All are similarly effective but do not produce the same effect. Whether the fuel is new or used, damp or dry, fine or coarse governs the results to a great extent. The temperature of the piece and the length of time it is in reduction also affect its final appearance. The strongest reduction will take place on the hottest piece—one completely buried in fine, new sawdust; the mildest reduction will develop on a cooler piece placed in a covered container of partly burned fuel. Damp fuel of any kind will have slight effect.

Pieces can be partially or entirely reduced; the results depend on how they are positioned in solid fuel. Patterns can be created by dropping leaves, wood chips, and the like on a piece at the proper moment—when reduction will take place immediately. These patterns are of a surface nature and because of their shallowness will reoxidize and disappear when the wood has burned. In fact, any reduction of the glaze or clay of a piece that is still hot will disappear when sufficient oxygen reaches it in the air. To make such effects lasting, the piece is plunged into water.

When water is not used to halt reoxidizing, the piece should be left in a reducing atmosphere for four or five minutes. It will then have cooled enough to be unaffected by the air. Decisions about reduction must be made in a matter of seconds; the potter must be able to act quickly while watching for planned or chance effects.

Plate being removed from charcoal kiln.

Plate's first contact with sawdust.

Controlling reduction with tongs. Note luster developing on plate at edge of sawdust.

Removing plate from sawdust.

Waving plate in air to partly reoxidize surface.

Plunging piece into water to hold desired effect.

Cleaning plate with mud.

Rinsing mud from plate.

Other changes may also be made on the piece when it is red hot. Often an unpleasant roughness results when inexperienced people are working with the process. They will put a piece in contact with sawdust when its glaze is still in a soft, molten condition. This may be undesirable in one instance, while in another it could be what the potter wants. Substances will stick or melt on a molten glaze, suggesting something dropped on its surface. Sand will stick, while borax, for example, may fuse onto the glaze.

Chemical changes resulting from contact between some materials and the molten glaze may be accomplished by bringing solutions of soluble salts of ceramic colors into contact with molten glaze. They may be poured, sprayed, dripped, or, with more control, put onto the pot with some tool. In combination with reduction, the following specific salts produce lusters: copper sulfate, antimony chloride, silver nitrate, tin chloride, and bismuth subnitrate. The heat of the piece and the duration of the reducing period combine to produce a variety of effects. Some of these effects in raku may be likened to the fuming of hand-blown glass.

All of these techniques are particularly appropriate to raku's philosophy of chance happening. A certain amount of control is exercised, but in the final analysis the results are, for the most part, due to elements and conditions outside the potter's precise control. Character can be repeated in successive pieces; specific duplication of other factors is impossible.

When the piece has cooled and can be handled, it is scrubbed with the hands or a sponge, and household cleanser or dirt. When washed thoroughly and dried, the raku piece is finished.

All of the techniques discussed in this chapter must be implemented within a three- or four-minute period. Often one will feel pressured to distraction. This is the moment of truth. But it can all be done over, with the same piece or a new one. This is *a* moment of truth!

Inevitably, raku is going to develop in ways not yet known. Insights and information have been presented here in the belief that further concepts and ideas will develop. There are many ways to see the many faces of raku.

A hot piece still steams after water quenching. An excellent raku form made by Estéban Prieto.

Plate by Gillian Hodge. A fine example of soft quality of raku in a thrown piece.
Silver nitrate was applied after firing and before reduction.

"Yin and Yang," a tile panel by the author, showing strong reduction and glaze inlay.

Selected Bibliography

Binns, Charles F. *The Potter's Craft.* New York: D. Van Nostrand, 1955.

Eppens-Van Veen, Joseph H. *Pottery.* New York: Universe Books, 1965.

Garzio, Angelo. "Raku." Ceramics Monthly Portfolio, 15.

Gilbertson, Warren. *Raku.* Columbus, Ohio: American Ceramic Society, 1943.

Leach, Bernard, *A Potter's Book.* Hollywood-by-the-Sea, Florida: Transatlantic Arts, 1967.

Rhodes, Daniel. *Clay and Glazes for the Potter.* New York: Chilton, 1957.

—— *Kilns: Design, Construction, and Operation.* New York: Chilton, 1969.

Riegger, Hal. "Raku." Ceramics Monthly Portfolio 7.

Index